Krishna Loves You

by Nishita Chaitanya

CHINMAYA BALA KATHA

Krishna loves you, don't you know?
Krishna loves you, don't you know?

Krishna loves you, don't you know?
Hurry now! Don't be slow . . .

Heavy and tired are your wee little eyes
To your toys now, say your goodbyes

Krishna loves you, don't you know?
He's right there by your soft pillow . .

Dancing Krishna jiggles into your bed
Snuggles up to you and strokes your head

Krishna loves you, don't you know?
In His eyes it really shows . . .

Caring Krishna gently kisses you goodnight
He makes everything amazingly all right

Krishna loves you, don't you know?
His smiles of sweetness glitter and glow . . .

Twinkle-eyed Krishna watches you dream
Of strawberries, custard, and ice cream

Krishna loves you, don't you know?
His curly locks swish and flow . . .

Laughing Krishna takes away your fears
Like a best friend whispering in your ears

Krishna loves you, don't you know?
Hear His flute play high and low . . .

At early dawn you stretch and rise
Hugging Krishna with your heart and eyes

Krishna loves you, don't you know?
So many times He's told you so!

Sunshine draws you into light
Oh, what a fun-tastic, magical night!

Krishna loves you, don't you know?
Just remember this as you go . . .

His masti, His charm, His never-ending grace
Oh, wow! That's put a big smile on your face!

Krishna loves you, don't you know?

Krishna loves you . . . now you know!

Krishna loves you, don't you know?

And I love Krishna, don't you know?